Using the Expressive Arts with Children and Young People Who Have Experienced Loss

This guidebook has been created to be used alongside the storybook, *The Girl Who Lost the Light in Her Eyes*. Using a relational approach, it explores the themes of the story and offers guidance to the adult as they use expressive arts to give the child or young person a creative outlet for their emotions. The gentle guidance offered makes this an ideal tool for non-specialists working with children experiencing loss or bereavement. It guides the adult to respond appropriately and sensitively to the grief of the child, whilst helping them journey through the grieving process.

This book must be used alongside the illustrated storybook, *The Girl Who Lost the Light in Her Eyes*. Both books are available to purchase as a set, *Supporting Children and Young People Who Experience Loss*. The full set includes:

- *The Girl Who Lost the Light in Her Eyes*, a colourfully illustrated and sensitively written storybook, designed to encourage conversation and support emotional literacy.
- *Using the Expressive Arts with Children and Young People Who Experience Loss*, a supporting guidebook that explores a relational approach and promotes creative expression as a way through loss or bereavement.

Perfectly crafted to spark communication around a difficult topic, this is an invaluable tool for practitioners, educators, parents, and anybody else looking to support a child or young person through loss or bereavement.

Juliette Ttofa is a specialist educational psychologist with a long-standing interest in the complex issues surrounding trauma, attachment needs and emotional resilience.

She specialises in supporting children and young people, their schools and families in understanding and responding to social, emotional and mental health needs through training, therapeutic support, and assessment and consultancy.

She is a Registered Sandplay Therapist and is passionate about using the expressive arts to support the mental health and wellbeing of all children and young people.

Using the Expressive Arts with Children and Young People Who Have Experienced Loss

A Pocket Guide

Juliette Ttofa

Routledge
Taylor & Francis Group

LONDON AND NEW YORK

First published 2021
by Routledge
2 Park Square, Milton Park, Abingdon, Oxon OX14 4RN

and by Routledge
52 Vanderbilt Avenue, New York, NY 10017

Routledge is an imprint of the Taylor & Francis Group, an informa business

British Library Cataloguing-in-Publication Data
A catalogue record for this book is available from the British Library

Library of Congress Cataloging-in-Publication Data
Names: Ttofa, Juliette, author.
Title: Using the expressive arts with children and young people who have experienced loss : a pocket guide / Juliette Ttofa.
Description: Abingdon, Oxon ; New York, NY : Routledge, 2020. | Includes bibliographical references.
Identifiers: LCCN 2020012787 (print) | LCCN 2020012788 (ebook) | ISBN 9780367524425 (paperback) | ISBN 9781003057994 (ebook)
Subjects: LCSH: Bereavement in children. | Bereavement in adolescence. | Arts—Therapeutic use.
Classification: LCC BF723.G75 T86 2020 (print) | LCC BF723.G75 (ebook) | DDC 155.9/37083—dc23
LC record available at https://lccn.loc.gov/2020012787
LC ebook record available at https://lccn.loc.gov/2020012788

ISBN: 978-0-367-52442-5 (pbk)
ISBN: 978-1-003-05799-4 (ebk)

Typeset in Calibri
by Apex CoVantage, LLC

Contents

Introduction

This pocket guide has been written to accompany the book *The Girl Who Lost the Light in Her Eyes*, which is a children's story about loss.

This guide aims to offer a relational approach, which can be used by adults to support children and young people through the new emotional landscape they may find themselves in following loss, in whatever form that takes.

Research has shown that a stable and supportive adult, who communicates empathy and compassion, is a powerful protective factor that can mitigate risk and help build the emotional resilience of a vulnerable child or young person (Ttofa, 2017).

A further aim of this guide is to support adults to use the expressive arts either non-directively, or directively in conjunction with the story book *The Girl Who Lost the Light in Her Eyes*.

A key message of this guide, therefore, is that creative expression and imagination, alongside a nurturing, trusted adult, are vitally important for supporting children's emotional wellbeing and resilience, especially during difficult times in their lives.

About loss

Most people will experience loss at some point in their lives and it can come in many forms. Loss can range from the loss of one's identity or *joie de vivre*, to the loss of a pet, a home, a trusted friend or member of the family. Sometimes multiple losses can occur at the same time.

Grief is usually used to describe the reaction to any form of loss, whilst bereavement may be specifically related to grief involving the death of a loved one.

Grief comes from the Latin word 'gravis', meaning heavy. Grief can feel this way – like carrying a heavy load that means it is hard for us to cope with even small, simple tasks throughout the day, let alone consider ways to recover our sense of joy. Francis Weller describes how we may feel estranged from the world following loss and begin to live as if close to the ground, the gravity of sorrow felt deep in our bones (Weller, 2015).

Weller explains how Scandinavian cultures describe the shift in their daily rhythms following grief as a time of 'living in the ashes', named after the tradition of spending days alongside the fires in the centre of a longhouse following a significant loss. This description acknowledges that when we experience loss, we may enter into an almost parallel but separate world. The individual remains in this physical and psychic space until they feel they have fully moved through the underworld journey that grief has taken them on.

This was the inspiration for the story *The Girl Who Lost the Light in Her Eyes*, which describes a journey through a parallel but separate kind of world – a 'time out of time' – to a place where sorrow is allowed and an emptying can take place.

In Scandinavian cultures, little is expected of those who are 'living in the ashes'. It is seen as a period of mourning and a time to go inwards in order to make sense of the experience of loss. Following this process, which can take a year or more, we may return deepened, wiser and changed. As Weller (2015: 22) says:

> What do we find there in the well of grief? Darkness, moistness that turns our eyes wet and our faces into streams of tears. We find the bodies of forgotten ancestors, abandoned dreams, ancient remnants of trees and animals—things that have come before and that have the power to lead us to the place to which each of us will return one day when we, too, leave this life, which has been gifted to us for a short time. This descent is a passage into what we are, creatures of earth.

Loss through the death of a loved one can be seismic for a child or young person. It can result in a wide range of feelings and emotions. It may also trigger old wounds to resurface. This kind of loss can be so destabilising and all-encompassing that it can be difficult for the child, and the adults around the child, to believe that their life will ever be joyful again.

Loss of a loved person is one of the most intensely painful experiences any human can suffer. Not only is it painful to experience but it is painful to witness.... To the bereaved nothing but the return of the lost person can bring them true comfort. (Bowlby, 1998: 7–8)

More than ever, there is a consensus that adverse childhood experiences (ACEs) such as loss or separation, and the potential unresolved trauma therein, may be associated with long-term physical and mental health difficulties if the young person is not supported to process or make sense of these experiences in a developmentally appropriate way.

Researchers have suggested different models for understanding how people cope with loss. In reality, everyone grieves in their own way and in their own time. No one way of grieving is better than any other.

These notes have therefore been designed as a simple, accessible guide for all adults supporting a child who has experienced loss.

Helping children and young people through loss

So, how can we help children and young people who have 'lost the light in their eyes'?

This guide puts forward a relational approach to helping children that is based upon strengthening our connection with them, alongside using expressive arts.

A relational approach encourages a trusted adult to validate and normalise the expressions of the child, rather than offer any interpretation or analysis. Moreover, this approach is a way of interacting with a child or young person that requires minimal resources.

A relational approach can be used alongside the expressive arts either directively or non-directively.

Note: The guide is not intended to replace any formal therapy that the child or young person might need. Rather, it is intended to support any adult working with the child to use the arts in a therapeutic way to ease and provide an outlet for their suffering.

Working non-directively using the expressive arts

The expressive arts have been used since the beginning of time to help human beings cope with the human condition.

Using our imagination alongside mark making can help us to create order and make sense of the often-chaotic world around us. It can also aid us in describing and communicating our complex inner world.

Offering a range of expressive arts activities for a young person to choose, in a non-directive manner, can be a helpful way to support a child during periods of adversity.

Working non-directively means providing a helping relationship where the child or young person feels valued, listened to and understood. As a result, the child has the chance to ruminate and reflect on their experiences, and ultimately make sense of their loss.

This might look like a weekly 30–50 minute Creative Workshop session between a child and trusted adult, with a range of expressive art materials on offer for the child to choose from.

Before you start: boundary setting

- Establish clear and consistent boundaries by ensuring the room you are in is free from distractions, having a few rules that you stick to and by creating a sense of routine e.g. where you will meet, when, why, for how long and what will happen each session.

- It is important from the outset to stress confidentiality and safeguarding duties when working with a child or young person in a setting.

Some suggested art materials

Drawing pencils, pencil crayons, paints and pastels

Mindful colouring books

Slime-making kit

Decopatch models

Air-drying clay, dough or modelling clay

Sandtray and miniature figures for storytelling

Writing materials – pen and ink

Other useful equipment

Paper, paint brushes,

Glue, scissors, water, aprons,

Paper towels, waterproof tablecloths

Using the expressive arts directively

Below are five exercises for using the storybook *The Girl Who Lost the Light in Her Eyes* therapeutically in a more directive way with a child or young person.

🖐 This symbol denotes some activities that can be used to expand on particular themes of the story. These are optional and their use will depend on the adult's knowledge of the child. The important thing is to use the arts to help give the young person an outlet for their emotions through imagination and creativity.

Read the story once through to the child or young person, then explore the themes of the story using these exercises:

Exercise 1: *'There was once a girl who lost the light in her eyes'*:
Encourage the child or young person to look at the face of the little
girl on the front cover and on the first page of the story book. Reflect
on how the girl might be feeling (e.g. sadness, hopelessness, despair)?
Use a range of 'emotions cards' or other emotional literacy resources
to help the child or young person.

✋ *Emotions portraits*: Invite the child to paint an image that
shows a difficult feeling or thought. This could be an abstract
picture or metaphor of the emotion, or a portrait of themselves
feeling the emotion.

Exercise 2: *'The light in one's eyes is difficult to paint ...'*: Invite the young person to look at the body language of the little girl on this page of the story and suggest what sensations she might be feeling in her body (e.g. tenseness, shut off, rigid etc). Emotion or mood cards can be used to help the young person to come up with more ideas.

✋ *Modelling clay animals*: Ask the child to create a clay or play dough model of an animal (or monster) that shows how they might act or look like in their body when they are experiencing a difficult feeling.

Exercise 3: '*Tears that told the story of her sadness*': Ask the child or young person why they think the girl in the story might be so sad. What is shown in her tears when she tells the story of her sadness? What did you think might be in the tears before you saw them? Here it might be helpful to talk about memories – and how memories can be bittersweet. We might remember the good times we had with a loved one with fondness, but we might also feel the sadness of losing them. Our own 'stories of sadness' might seem to take us backwards, but they can also help us to move forwards, whilst keeping a special place for these memories within our heart. In short, to heal, we need to feel. And we also need to feel heard.

A teardrops timeline: Invite the child or young person to think about what might be in their tears if 'the painter boy' drew tears for them. The child or young person can write or draw their own story or timeline inside large blank tear drops that form a sequence. Alternatively, they may wish to tell a story using a sandtray and miniature figures.

Exercise 4: *'And then he noticed it, shining like the light at the end of a dark tunnel ...'*: Invite the child or young person to consider what has come back to the little girl at the end of the story (this could be an emotion, a memory or an important value or strength like friendship). How might she be feeling when the sparkle of light returns to her eyes? (e.g. joy, happiness, enthusiasm, radiance, liveliness, exuberance, delight, spiritedness, energy etc).

> ✋ *Strengths stones*: Paint pebbles in different colours and write 'strengths' words or values onto them in pen. These are strengths the child or young person can hold onto in difficult times. Use 'strengths cards' to help the young person to think of strengths important to them.

Exercise 5: *The blue bird*: There is a small blue bird in the book. Can you follow it through the story? What do you think this blue bird symbolises? (e.g. hope, faith, truth, trust, imagination etc).

🖐 *Affirmation bunting*: Invite the child to think of what gives them hope and makes them feel happy. This could be a positive statement or affirmation linked to one of their strengths, or something they enjoy doing, or a person or a place (e.g. 'I am creative', 'I like playing', 'I enjoy reading', 'I love my family', 'I love my friends', 'I am happy when it's sunny'). Write each of these onto colourful, triangle-shaped pieces of paper and attach to a ribbon to create the child's own positive affirmation bunting.

Using the expressive arts S.A.F.E.L.Y.

There are a few considerations to keep in mind when using the expressive arts with a child or young person. These are summarised using the acronym 'S.A.F.E.L.Y.' below:

1. Safe space

It is vital when working with a child or young person to establish safety and trust, first and foremost. Within this safe and trusted relationship, the child or young person will feel valued, and, as a result, they will be more open to self-expression.

This includes not interpreting any metaphors expressed or trying to fix their pain, but simply being there to hear and see what the child communicates. If the supporting adult jumps straight to analysing, interpreting or fixing a problem, the child or young person may not feel heard or seen.

This might look like *letting the child know they are safe and that you are there for them, thanking the young person for sharing their art with you, admitting that you don't know what to say* and you *can't fix things.*

It is also important to ensure that you keep anything the child or young person creates safe (e.g. in a folder or box).

2. <u>A</u>ttune to and accept the child

The key role of an adult who is supporting a child or young person is to attune to the child and be accepting of their emotions.

The adult's role is also to focus on what the child or young person is communicating, to warmly receive and encourage the child's emotional responses, and to validate and normalise this expression, rather than dismiss it or show disapproval.

Much of this may be non-verbal, for example, being still and present for the child or young person in the moment, attending to the child, turning towards them, looking interested, listening actively, pausing to let them talk, giving them space and time, and showing them increased attention and emotional warmth.

This increased attunement and emotional warmth can help to provide the child or young person with a buffer for the adversity they have experienced, restoring a sense of balance and supporting their ability to be resilient.

3. Follow the child's lead

When using the expressive arts with a young person, it is desirable to follow their lead and to trust that they know what they need to heal. Our role is to be curious about what direction the child might wish to take and to provide the free time and protected space for this to unfold.

Experiencing difficult feelings is sometimes described as like being stuck in a dark tunnel. Rather than becoming immobilised or overwhelmed by the emotions we are experiencing, we need to allow ourselves to feel the energy of the emotion, in order to get to the light at the end of the tunnel.

But we, as adults, cannot direct or force the young person through the tunnel at our pace.

Children and young people need the support of a trusted adult to metaphorically walk alongside them – to hold onto hope, like a lantern, so that they will find their way through the darkness of complex emotions, and make their own way out of the tunnel, in their own time.

This does not mean that there is no direction, but that the direction comes from the child.

4. <u>E</u>mpathy is healing

Having an adult who communicates empathy whilst a child or young person uses the expressive arts, supports their ability to allow expression for the emotions associated with painful experiences.

The adult's role is to show that they are feeling with the child or young person, when emotional expression arises so that the child can accept all feelings as normal.

The adult can demonstrate empathy by tuning into the child's body language, facial expression and gestures and using empathic verbal or non-verbal responses.

 Some suggested verbal responses:

"I can see how very difficult this is/has been for you."

"That sounds so hard ..."

"I am so sorry you are going through this."

"Of course you are going to feel X, I would too if that had happened to me ..."

"No wonder you are upset ..."

Over time, by describing stressful experiences to an empathic adult, a child or young person will feel less alone. This can be healing in itself.

5. Listen to the child and label any feelings that arise

A trusted adult can provide time to listen to the child or young person and try to understand what they are feeling.

If any feelings are expressed in the course of using expressive arts, the adult supporting the child or young person can firstly child check their own understanding of the child's emotional responses and then in turn help the child to better recognize, understand, label and express their own feelings.

The child or young person can be given opportunities to name their emotions using simple words, (or if appropriate, using relevant books or emotions cards).

Once emotions are labelled, it may be easier to let them go. When we label a child's feelings, we also communicate to the child that they are understood by those around them.

With compassionate listening and understanding, the child or young person will feel more supported during this difficult time.

6. Yes to expression

It is the role of the trusted adult to encourage expression from the child or young person.

Expression is vital for healing. The more we can support young people to express their distress, rather than suppress it, the more they will engage in a positive feedback loop that ultimately leads to greater resilience to stress or adversity.

Suppression on the other hand can lead to withdrawal, vulnerability and a negative feedback loop that may result in unhealthy outcomes for the child.

In the absence of any words or expression for emotional experiences, a child or young person may put a lid on their feelings and become distant or detached. Alternatively, they may discharge their feelings through unhelpful or unhealthy behaviours.

But through expressive arts, the child can begin to reorganize their thoughts and emotions and gain a greater sense of coherence and meaning about life events. This can also help to instil a sense of hope in young people, whilst also supporting their self-regulation skills.

Our role as the trusted adult, is to help the child to view distress as something human, but temporary, that needs expression in order for us to heal.

And finally ... a brave new world

One of the most challenging aspects of loss is adjusting to a new reality.

Adjusting may require a child or young person to rethink their future. They may even adopt a new sense of identity following a significant loss. Solution-focused or strengths-based work may be needed to help the child to identify new goals and develop new friendships and connections.

As part of bereavement support or counselling, a new daily ritual and routine may be discussed, such as a daily (or weekly) practice to pause for reflection in a special place.

Coping skills or *self-care techniques* may be discussed as part of a wider plan of help and support. The child or young person may come up with their own ideas for calming strategies e.g. mindful breathing, nurturing sensory experiences, exercise or physical activities, and spending time in nature or with animals.

A useful *ongoing activity* to suggest to a young person who has experienced loss might be to encourage them to keep a 'Feelings Diary' or a 'Dream's Diary'.

Finally, the young person may need additional nurture, support and formal therapy to *maintain their resilience.*

References

Bowlby, J. (1998 [1980]). *Attachment and Loss Volume 3: Loss: Sadness and Depression*. London: Pimlico.

Ttofa, J. (2017). *Nurturing Emotional Resilience in Vulnerable Children and Young People: A Practical Guide*. London: Routledge.

Weller, F. (2015) *The Wild Edge of Sorrow: Rituals of Renewal and the Sacred Work of Grief*. Berkeley, CA: North Atlantic Books.